BIOGRAPHIC
EINSTEIN

BIOGRAPHIC
EINSTEIN

BRIAN CLEGG

AMMONITE
PRESS

First published 2018 by
Ammonite Press
an imprint of Guild of Master Craftsman Publications Ltd
Castle Place, 166 High Street, Lewes, East Sussex, BN7 1XU,
United Kingdom
www.ammonitepress.com

ISBN 978 1 78145 333 9

A catalogue record for this book is available from the
British Library.

Publisher: Jason Hook
Concept Design: Matt Carr
Design & Illustration: Matt Carr & Robin Shields
Editor: Jamie Pumfrey

Colour reproduction by GMC Reprographics
Printed and bound in Turkey

CONTENTS

ICONOGRAPHIC

WHEN WE CAN RECOGNIZE A SCIENTIST BY A SET OF ICONS, WE CAN ALSO RECOGNIZE HOW COMPLETELY THAT SCIENTIST AND THEIR THEORIES HAVE ENTERED OUR CULTURE AND OUR CONSCIOUSNESS.

INTRODUCTION

There has never been another scientist in history who has quite captured people's imagination in the way Albert Einstein did. The image of his shock of white hair is enough to conjure up a picture of a great thinker with a distinct sense of humour. And Einstein's place in the scientific hall of fame is entirely justified. Few others can claim to have contributed so much to the foundations of a scientific field. Modern physics rests on two pillars – relativity and quantum theory – and Einstein was involved in the development of both.

Einstein's defining characteristic was probably his rejection of authority. At 15 he was expelled from school. Not long after, at an age when most teenagers would have few concerns beyond education and relationships, he was working out how to renounce his German citizenship. A lifelong pacifist, he was appalled at Germany's requirement for him to do a year's military service.

"I NEVER THINK OF THE FUTURE. IT COMES SOON ENOUGH."

—Albert Einstein, December 1930

After scraping through a degree – because he only bothered to attend lectures on topics that interested him – Einstein could not get an academic post and ended up spending seven years as a clerk in the Swiss patent office. For anyone else, this might have seemed the end of their scientific career, but while at the patent office, in 1905, Einstein published his PhD thesis and four remarkable papers. One established the existence of atoms and molecules, a second laid the foundations for quantum theory (later winning him the Nobel Prize), the third introduced the world to the special theory of relativity and the fourth pointed out that $E=mc^2$.

This flurry of excellence inevitably led to academic posts, where Einstein was never a particularly enthusiastic teacher. But, over eight years between 1907 and 1915, he assembled what would be his masterpiece. The general theory of relativity showed how matter influenced space and time, and how space and time in return influenced the way that matter moved. At its simplest, general relativity made sense of the force of gravity – but it would do far more, from predicting the existence of black holes to shaping the history of the universe.

"THE MOST INCOMPREHENSIBLE THING ABOUT THE WORLD IS THAT IT IS COMPREHENSIBLE."

—Albert Einstein, *Albert Einstein: Creator and Rebel*, 1972

By this time, Einstein's marriage to his first wife, Mileva, was nearing its end. He had met Mileva, a fellow physics student, at university and at first their relationship had been strong. They had three children; the first, Lieserl, was probably adopted at birth as there is no further record of her. The others, Hans Albert and Eduard, born after Einstein got his first job, stayed with Mileva, increasingly left behind as Einstein's career took off. In 1919, Mileva agreed to a divorce provided she got the Nobel Prize money, should Einstein ever win it.

All of this involved a very different Einstein to the iconic pictures – a dapper young man with short, dark hair. But his second marriage to his cousin Elsa began another phase of his life when the familiar "absent-minded professor" persona developed. Once Einstein had moved to the USA in 1933 to escape the Nazi regime, his transformation was complete. But we always should remember that fame came to the dashing young man, not the elder statesman.

"IF A IS A SUCCESS IN LIFE, THEN A EQUALS X PLUS Y PLUS Z. WORK IS X; Y IS PLAY; AND Z IS KEEPING YOUR MOUTH SHUT."

—Albert Einstein,
The Observer, 1950

ALBERT EINSTEIN

01
LIFE

"SCIENCE IS THE ATTEMPT TO MAKE THE CHAOTIC DIVERSITY OF OUR SENSE-EXPERIENCE CORRESPOND TO A LOGICALLY UNIFORM SYSTEM OF THOUGHT."

—Albert Einstein, *Out of My Later Years,* 1950

ALBERT EINSTEIN

was born on 14 March 1879 in Ulm, southern Germany

OLGASTRASSE

KELTERGASSE

SEDELHOFGASSE

RAILWAY
STATION

FRIEDRICH-EBERT-STRASSE

BAHNHOFPL.

BAHNHOFSTRASSE

Young Albert would not spend long in the city of Ulm, where he was born in an apartment building that would be destroyed during the Second World War. Ulm is located on the Danube, near the border with Bavaria in the German state of Württemberg. Here, Albert's father, Hermann, and two of Hermann's cousins ran a feather-bed shop together. In 1880, the Einsteins moved to Munich to join Hermann's brother Jakob in setting up a larger business making electrical equipment. Though Jewish, the Einsteins were not religious and would later send Albert to a Catholic school.

GERMANY

ULM

MUNICH

Also born
in Ulm:
composer
EUGEN HAILE
(1873–1933)

CANADA

Inventor Sandford Fleming proposes universal time with time zones.

UK

Female students are admitted at Oxford University, though they are not yet able to receive a degree.

USA

The Church of Christ, Scientist (Christian Scientists) is founded.

THE WORLD IN
1879

USA

Thomas Edison gives a public display of his first effective light bulb.

CHILE

Chile declares war on Bolivia and Peru over the ownership of the Atacama Desert.

Germany itself was newly established as a nation, founded in 1871 as an amalgamation of sovereign states. Dominated by the northern Prussian states, the southern states – where the Einsteins lived – felt less part of the whole, and Württemberg still felt more of a separate entity than a region of the burgeoning German empire. The Einstein family's world was primarily shaped by the successes and failures (frankly, mostly failures) of Hermann Einstein's business career. It would see them later move to another south German state and then, in Albert's teens, to Italy in an attempt to keep the business afloat.

DENMARK

Henrik Ibsen's play *A Doll's House* premieres in Copenhagen.

RUSSIA

Tchaikovsky's opera *Eugene Onegin* premieres.

GERMANY

The first electric passenger train runs at the Berlin Trades Exposition.

BULGARIA

The Bulgaria National Bank is founded.

GERMANY

The chemical company Linde is formed.

SOUTH AFRICA

The Anglo-Zulu War begins.

GRANDMOTHER

Jette Bernheimer
(1825–86)

GRANDFATHER

Julius Dörzbacher
(1816–95)

MOTHER

Pauline Koch
(1858–1920)

FIRST WIFE

Mileva Marić
(1875–1948)

Albert Einstein
(1879–1955)

DAUGHTER

Lieserl Einstein
(1902–d. unknown)

SON

Hans Albert Einstein
(1904–73)

SON

Eduard Einstein
(1910–65)

GRANDMOTHER

Helene Moos
(1814–87)

GRANDFATHER

Abraham Einstein
(1808–68)

FATHER

Hermann Einstein
(1847–1902)

SISTER

Maja Einstein
(1881–1951)

THE EINSTEINS

SECOND WIFE

Elsa Einstein
(1876–1936)

Albert's mother, Pauline Koch, was born in Cannstatt, one of the districts of the capital of Württemberg, Stuttgart. His father, Hermann, came from Buchau, a much smaller nearby town, though one that was considered important due to its historical roots as one of the Holy Roman Empire's Free Imperial Cities. The Koch family (Pauline's father changed his name from the original Dörzbacher) was the more affluent of the two by a long way – Pauline's father was a self-made corn merchant of some standing and helped fund Hermann's business. Albert's second wife, Elsa, was both his first and second cousin – their mothers were sisters, and their fathers were cousins.

EARLY LIFE

Young Albert's family life was a happy one – he had loving parents and got on well with his younger sister – but his home life contrasted significantly with his experience of school. Being in education certainly boosted his independence – his parents even let him walk to school on his own from the age of four, though they did initially follow to keep an eye on him. But his insistence on doing things his own way often resulted in bad relations with the staff, famously resulting in him being told by a teacher that he would "never amount to anything".

Albert attends Catholic elementary school.

He begins playing the violin.

1879 | 1880 | 1881 | 1882 | 1883 | 1884 | 1885 | 1886 | 1887

Albert Einstein is born on 14 March at his parents' home in Ulm, Germany.

Albert's sister Maria, known as Maja, is born.

The Einstein family move to Munich where Albert's father Hermann sets up a company with Albert's uncle Jakob.

Albert is off school ill for several weeks – his father gives him a compass to play with, which fascinates him.

Albert discovers Mozart and his violin playing goes from being a chore to a delight.

Albert takes the entrance exams for the Swiss Federal Polytechnic (ETH) in Zürich, but fails.

1888 1889 1890 1891 1892 1893 1894 1895 1896

The Einstein family move to Pavia in Italy to pursue new business opportunities. Albert remains at school in Munich.

Albert spends a year at a Swiss school, falls in love with the principal's daughter and gives up his German citizenship.

Einstein moves to the Luitpold Gymnasium, where he is educated to the age of 15.

Albert quits school (only to be told he is already expelled) and heads for Italy to rejoin the family.

TONIGHT ONLY: EINSTEIN AND THE RELATIVITIES

There is one musical instrument inextricably linked to Albert Einstein – the violin. Einstein was never a practical scientist – his laboratory equipment comprised paper and pencil – but he certainly demonstrated dexterity with his violin playing. It didn't start well. When his mother, herself an enthusiastic pianist, engaged his first teacher, the five-year-old refused to play, flying into such a dramatic rage that the teacher wouldn't stay. Luckily, after a second teacher was found, Einstein became a competent violinist. He claimed his love of playing began when he discovered Mozart's sonatas at the age of 13. He also enjoyed playing the piano. Einstein isn't the only great scientist to have shown a talent for music ...

FROM LEFT TO RIGHT: EINSTEIN ON VIOLIN, BRIAN COX ON SYNTHESIZER, BRIAN MAY ON GUITAR, RICHARD FEYNMAN ON BONGOS AND MAX PLANCK ON PIANO

CHASING A BEAM OF LIGHT

One of the most interesting things about the way Einstein worked is that he largely developed his theories in his head. Using just his mind, he was able to conceptualize ideas through the use of thought experiments. In 1896, Einstein enrolled at a Swiss school whose educational principles had been revolutionized by Johann Heinrich Pestalozzi. Pestalozzi's motto, "Learning by head, hand and heart," encouraged visualizing concepts and its impact on Einstein is obvious. In his 1955 autobiography, *Autobiographische Skizze*, Einstein recalled: "During this year in Aarau, the following question came to me: if one chases a light wave with the speed of light, one would have in front of him a time independent wave field. Such a thing seems however not to exist!" This was Einstein's first thought experiment and would form the basis for what would later become his theory of special relativity. As Einstein's career progressed, he would continue to use thought experiments to revolutionize modern physics.

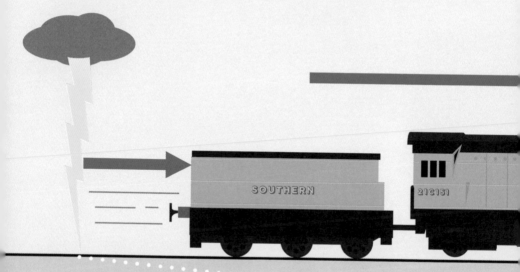

EINSTEIN'S TRAIN

One of Einstein's early thought experiments examined the idea of simultaneity, the relation between two events which are assumed to be happening at the same time. According to Einstein, events that are simultaneous for one observer may not be for another depending on the state of motion.

> ## "IMAGINATION IS MORE IMPORTANT THAN KNOWLEDGE. FOR KNOWLEDGE IS LIMITED, WHEREAS IMAGINATION EMBRACES THE ENTIRE WORLD, STIMULATING PROGRESS, GIVING BIRTH TO EVOLUTION. IT IS, STRICTLY SPEAKING, A REAL FACTOR IN SCIENTIFIC RESEARCH."

—Albert Einstein, *Cosmic Religion: With Other Opinions and Aphorisms*, 1931

EINSTEIN EXPRESS

In the experiment, Einstein imagined two bolts of lightning striking train tracks at the same time, but at either end of a train. Now, if a passenger is sitting in the middle of the train, and the train is moving forward at a very high speed, by the time the light arrives to them, they will be closer to the lightning bolt at the front. The passenger would then believe that it happened first. However, if an observer was standing beside the tracks, midway between the two strikes, they will claim that they struck simultaneously. Einstein realized that two people in relative motion experience time differently, meaning that simultaneity is relative.

ADULTHOOD

Einstein's adult life had two distinct phases. From going to university at the Swiss Federal Polytechnic (ETH) to leaving Germany for good, he moved around frequently. Once he had left the patent office, he held university positions in several European countries, and during this period he did all his best work. His marriage failed, but was followed very quickly with a second to Elsa Einstein. The second phase began after moving to the USA. Although he would travel for talks and events, Einstein never left his home in Princeton, New Jersey. He continued to work to the end of his life, but would not achieve further major breakthroughs.

1903

Einstein marries Mileva Marić. Employed in the patent office in Bern.

1896

On his second attempt, Einstein enrols at the Swiss Federal Polytechnic (ETH), in Zürich.

1902

Einstein's daughter Lieserl is born. It is assumed she was adopted or died as there is no further record of her.

1900

Having graduated from ETH, Einstein is awarded his teaching diploma.

1901

Einstein gains Swiss citizenship.

1904

Einstein and Mileva's first son, Hans Albert, is born – he will become a professor of engineering.

1910

The couple's third child, Eduard, is born.

1914

Einstein and Mileva separate. She moves to Zürich, taking Eduard and Hans Albert with her.

1919

Having been apart for over five years, Einstein and Mileva finally divorce. In the same year, Albert marries Elsa Löwenthal.

1955

Einstein dies in Princeton Hospital from an aortic aneurysm.

1940

Einstein becomes a citizen of the USA.

1936

After Elsa dies, Einstein is looked after by his secretary, Helen Dukas.

1933

Einstein moves to the USA, settling in Princeton, New Jersey.

THE PATENT OFFICE

In 1900, Einstein graduated from university in Zurich and began searching for full-time employment. After two years without any luck, he was finally offered a position as a 'technical expert' at the patent office in Bern, 60 miles (96 km) away. For many would-be scientists failing to get an academic position, the job at the patent office would have been a dead end. But Einstein found the job easy and it allowed him time to think and produce his first published academic papers as well as finish off his doctoral thesis. It's even likely the work inspired his thinking on special relativity, which was all about how space and time interacted. In his job, Einstein handled several patents on synchronizing railway clocks using the electric telegraph, which transformed communication timescales. He often illustrated relativity with examples of railway tracks and synchronizing clocks.

DISTANCE = 60 MILES (96 KM)

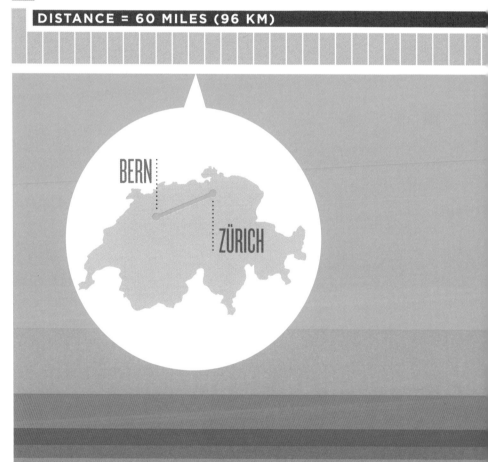

BERN

ZÜRICH

The telegraph transformed communication timescales between cities. This graphic shows how long it would take to communicate between Zurich – where Einstein graduated – and Bern – where he worked on patents – using the telegraph and other methods.

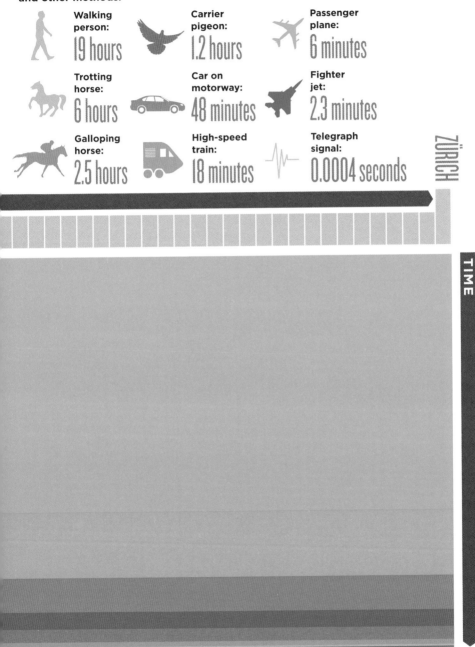

Walking person:
19 hours

Carrier pigeon:
1.2 hours

Passenger plane:
6 minutes

Trotting horse:
6 hours

Car on motorway:
48 minutes

Fighter jet:
2.3 minutes

Galloping horse:
2.5 hours

High-speed train:
18 minutes

Telegraph signal:
0.0004 seconds

ZÜRICH

TIME

LIFE

THE TRAVELLING PHYSICIST

Most academics travel from place to place as their career builds, but in the early 1900s it was rare for a teenager like Einstein to be such an international citizen. Having briefly experienced life in Italy with his parents and found that it was not for him – and with his German citizenship renounced – it seemed as if he would settle in Switzerland. However, once he gained academic credibility Einstein bounced around a number of central European states before settling back in Germany. Hitler's rise meant that Einstein was forced to move again. After considering the UK, he opted for the USA, where the research-only Institute for Advanced Study proved an ideal academic home.

Ulm, Germany (1879–80)
Birthplace

Munich, Germany (1880–94)
Childhood

Pavia, Italy (1894–95)
First experience outside Germany

Aarau, Switzerland (1895–96)
Secondary education and first love

Zürich, Switzerland (1896–1902)
University

Bern, Switzerland (1902–09)
Patent office job, first marriage and first academic post

Zürich, Switzerland (1909–11)
Associate professor at the University
of Zürich

Prague, Czechoslovakia (1911–12)
Full professor at Karl-Ferdinand
University

Zürich, Switzerland (1912–14)
Professor at his alma mater, ETH

Berlin, Germany (1914–33)
General relativity, international fame
and second marriage

New York City, USA (1921)
First visit to the USA

New York & Pasadena, USA (1930–31)
Second visit to the USA

De Haan, Belgium (1933)
Safe haven from Germany and the
rise of Hitler

London, England (1933)
Persuades Winston Churchill to help
Jewish scientists in Germany, but his
attempt to get British citizenship fails

Princeton, USA (1933–55)
Professor at the Institute for Advanced
Study and US citizenship

EINSTEIN'S BRAIN

Ever since the brain was identified as the centre of intelligence, people have wondered if great thinkers have especially large or complex brains. The pathologist who performed Einstein's autopsy kept the brain (without the permission of the family), photographed it and cut it into over 240 blocks, which were preserved in a plastic-like substance called collodion and stored in alcohol. The pieces were found in two jars inside a cider box over 20 years later. Although several small oddities have been claimed, notably a larger region dealing with visual processing, there is no good evidence that Einstein's brain was markedly different from a typical human brain.

Average brain weights:

1 YEAR OLD
0.8kg

WOMAN
1.22kg

ALBERT EINSTEIN
1.23kg

MAN
1.35kg

CHIMPANZEE
420g

RAVEN
15g

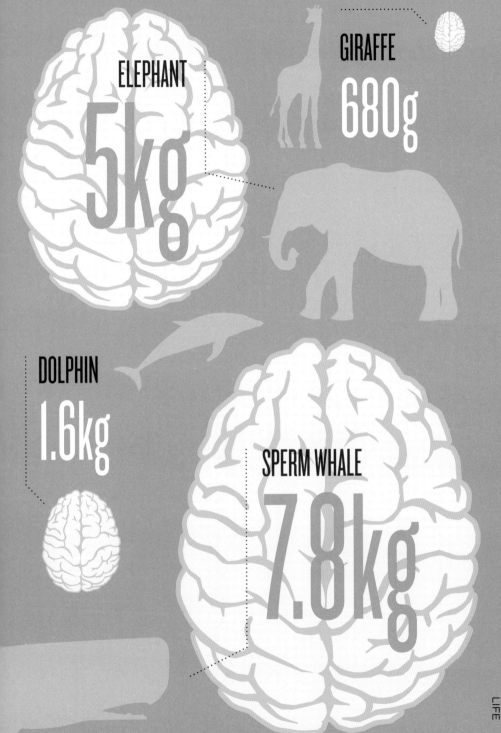

ELEPHANT
5kg

GIRAFFE
680g

DOLPHIN
1.6kg

SPERM WHALE
7.8kg

DEATH OF A GENIUS

Einstein was admitted to Princeton Hospital in New Jersey on 15 April 1955 with what was described at the time as an "internal complaint". He had had an abdominal aortic aneurysm reinforced in 1948 but chose to not undergo further surgery and died when it ruptured. At his request, his ashes were scattered, but decidedly against his wishes and without the family's permission, his eyes and his brain were kept by the hospital pathologist, Thomas Stoltz Harvey. The eyes were given to Einstein's optometrist Henry Abrams and remain in a deposit box in New York. The brain, cut into sections, was stored after examination and only relinquished in 1997.

DATE:
18 APRIL 1955

AGE: 76

CAUSE OF DEATH:

Abdominal aortic
aneurysm

LAST WORDS:

Mumbled in German
and not understood
or recorded

TOMBSTONE:

Einstein asked
that his ashes
be scattered in
an undisclosed
location so that
his tomb did not
become a shrine

"NO OTHER MAN CONTRIBUTED SO MUCH TO THE VAST EXPANSION OF 20TH-CENTURY KNOWLEDGE. YET NO OTHER MAN WAS MORE MODEST IN THE POSSESSION OF THE POWER THAT IS KNOWLEDGE, MORE SURE THAT POWER WITHOUT WISDOM IS DEADLY. TO ALL WHO LIVE IN THE NUCLEAR AGE, ALBERT EINSTEIN EXEMPLIFIED THE MIGHTY CREATIVE ABILITY OF THE INDIVIDUAL IN A FREE SOCIETY."

—President Dwight D.
Eisenhower's statement
on Einstein's death, 1955

ALBERT EINSTEIN

02
WORLD

"CULTURE IN ITS HIGHEST FORMS IS A DELICATE PLANT WHICH DEPENDS ON A COMPLICATED SET OF CONDITIONS AND IS WONT TO FLOURISH ONLY IN A FEW PLACES AT ANY GIVEN TIME."

—Albert Einstein, *The World As I See It*, 1949

CLASSICAL PHYSICS

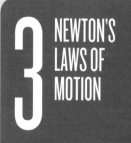

- **Mechanics**
- **Newton's laws of motion**
- **Optics**
- **Acoustics**
- **Thermodynamics**
- **Electrodynamics**
- **Electromagnetism**
- **Fluid dynamics**

3 NEWTON'S LAWS OF MOTION

I. A body at rest will remain at rest, and a body in motion will remain in motion unless it is acted upon by an external force.

II. The force acting on an object is equal to the mass of that object times its acceleration.

III. For every action there is an equal and opposite reaction.

MODERN PHYSICS

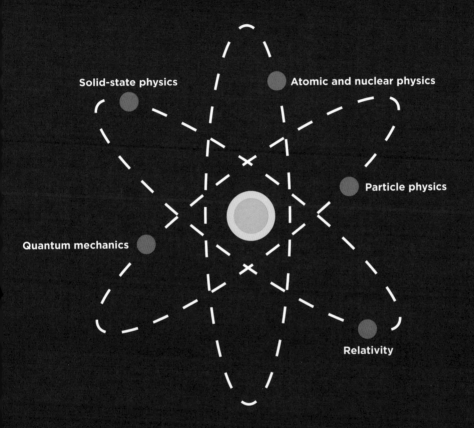

Solid-state physics

Atomic and nuclear physics

Particle physics

Quantum mechanics

Relativity

At the end of the 19th century, physics was still limited by its established foundations, developed over 2,000 years by scientists such as Issac Newton, Galileo and Michael Faraday. Classical physics addressed the observable: speeds less than the speed of light and sizes greater than that of atoms, including the study of motion and the basic understandings of the universe. It's often reported that in 1900, British physicist Lord Kelvin stated, "there is nothing new to be discovered in physics now. All that remains is more and more precise measurement," though there's no proof he ever said this. However, in 1905, Einstein's groundbreaking work on relativity opened up the possibility that physics was not complete, which paved the way for modern physics. In contrast to classical physics, modern physics looks at very high speeds and minute distances, and includes nuclear physics and quantum theory. In its simplest form, classical physics can be defined as the work dating up to the 20th century, while modern physics looks at post-1900 physics up until the present.

SCIENTIFIC DISCOVERIES OF THE 20TH CENTURY

WALTER SUTTON AND THEODOR BOVERI SUGGEST THAT CHROMOSOMES CARRY HEREDITARY INFORMATION
1902

ALBERT EINSTEIN PROVES THE EXISTENCE AND THE SIZE OF ATOMS AND MOLECULES, PROPOSES THE PHOTOELECTRIC EFFECT, AND SUGGESTS SPECIAL THEORY OF RELATIVITY AND THE EQUATION $E=mc^2$
1905

ERNEST RUTHERFORD DISCOVERS ATOMIC STRUCTURE
1911

NIELS BOHR PROPOSES QUANTUM THEORY OF THE ATOM
1913

EDWIN HUBBLE REVEALS THE UNIVERSE IS MORE THAN THE MILKY WAY
1923

It's easy to confuse fame with outstanding contribution to science. Some scientists are better known for their media exposure than their work – and Einstein was arguably the biggest celebrity scientist since Newton. In both these cases, however, the fame was warranted. Just as Newton was at the heart of transforming 17th-century science, Einstein contributed to the two great breakthroughs of 20th-century physics. This doesn't mean, though, that Einstein's was the only significant contribution to 20th-century scientific knowledge. The century saw a transformation in the way we approach science and understand everything, from the universe as a whole to the mechanisms of life.

GEORGES LEMAÎTRE SHOWS UNIVERSE IS EXPANDING
1927

ALEXANDER FLEMING DISCOVERS PENICILLIN
1928

JAMES WATSON AND FRANCIS CRICK REVEAL THE STRUCTURE OF DNA
1953

ARNO PENZIAS AND ROBERT WILSON DETECT COSMIC MICROWAVE BACKGROUND, SOMETIMES CALLED THE "ECHO" OF THE BIG BANG
1964

DARK ENERGY, ACCELERATING THE EXPANSION OF THE UNIVERSE, IS FOUND
1998

SCIENCE AND RELIGION

Einstein held no specific religious faith, but liked the idea of a non-interfering 'God in everything', which he sometimes called 'the old one'. He claimed he was not an atheist, but an agnostic. Apart from his famous quote, "God does not play dice with the universe," expressing his distaste for the probabilistic aspects of quantum theory, his best-known comments featuring God form a pair of bookends for his attitude to life. He said in 1921, "Raffiniert ist der Herrgott, aber boshaft ist er nicht," often translated as "The Lord God is subtle, but malicious he is not" – though his own favoured version was "God is slick, but he ain't mean." Somewhat later in life, however, he remarked, "I have second thoughts. Maybe God is malicious." Science and faith are often pitted against each other, but as the graphic shows, the two do overlap.

CHARLES BABBAGE
RENÉ DESCARTES
MICHAEL FARADAY
GALILEO GALILEI
WERNER HEISENBERG
ANTONY HEWISH
LORD KELVIN
GEORGES LEMAÎTRE
JAMES CLERK MAXWELL
ISAAC NEWTON
MAX PLANCK
ABDUS SALAM

- Believers
- Agnostics and waverers
- Atheists

DAVID ATTENBOROUGH
FRANCIS CRICK
MARIE CURIE
CHARLES DARWIN
ALBERT EINSTEIN
ENRICO FERMI
ROSALIND FRANKLIN
MURRAY GELL-MANN
MARTIN REES

NIELS BOHR
RICHARD DAWKINS
PAUL DIRAC
RICHARD FEYNMAN
EDMOND HALLEY
STEPHEN HAWKING
FRED HOYLE
LINUS PAULING
ERWIN SCHRÖDINGER
JAMES WATSON

THE BORN LETTERS

Einstein and the German physicist Max Born were friends for more than 40 years, and for much of this time kept up a steady correspondence that mixed comments on their scientific ideas with more everyday observations. Born, who was grandfather to the famous singer Olivia Newton-John, worked on quantum physics alongside Heisenberg and Schrödinger. One of his biggest contributions to the field was his realization that Schrödinger's wave equation did not describe the location of a particle but rather the probability of finding it in a particular location. Because Born put probability at the heart of quantum theory, it was to him that Einstein addressed some of his best-known criticisms.

114 LETTERS

- from Einstein to Max Born
- from Einstein to Max and his wife Hedi
- from Max Born to Einstein
- from Einstein to Hedi Born
- from Max and Hedi Born to Einstein

◀ **Max Born was a German physicist and mathematician who was instrumental in the development of quantum mechanics.**

1924 EINSTEIN TO THE BORNS

"I find the idea quite intolerable that an electron exposed to radiation should choose of its own free will, not only its moment to jump off but its direction. In that case, I would rather be a cobbler, or even an employee in a gaming house, than a physicist."

EINSTEIN TO BORN 1926

"Quantum mechanics is certainly imposing. But an inner voice tells me that it is not yet the real thing. The theory says a lot, but does not really bring us any closer to the secret of the 'old one'. I, at any rate, am convinced that He is not playing at dice."

1933 EINSTEIN TO BORN

"I've been promoted to an 'evil monster' in Germany, and all my money has been taken away from me. But I console myself with the thought that the latter would soon be gone anyway."

EINSTEIN TO BORN 1936

"Together with a young collaborator, I arrived at the interesting result that gravitational waves do not exist." (He would later change his mind again.)

1947 EINSTEIN TO BORN

"I cannot seriously believe in [the current quantum theory] because the theory cannot be reconciled with the idea that physics should represent a reality in time and space, free from spooky actions at a distance."

EINSTEIN AND THE BOMB

It all started with E=mc², or m=L/V², as Einstein wrote the equation in his 1905 paper (L is energy released and V the speed of light). Einstein suggested his idea might be tested with radioactive radium salts, but had no idea of a practical application for his work. By 1939, though, with the development of nuclear chain reactions and fission, Einstein was persuaded to go against his pacifist beliefs to sign a letter urging US President Roosevelt to sanction work on nuclear weapons in response to the threat that Germany may do the same. Einstein later expressed his regret for signing the letter, and for its outcome.

HIGH EXPLOSIVE

V-2 ROCKET (1944)

The world's first long-range guided ballistic missile.

FISSION

LITTLE BOY (1945)

First atomic bomb used in war. Dropped on Hiroshima in Japan.

W73 (1978)

Smallest Trident II missile fission warhead.

THERMONUCLEAR

CASTLE BRAVO (1954)

Largest thermonuclear bomb detonated by the USA.

DISTANCE OF EFFECT

0.004 mi² (0.01 km

4.4 mi (11.4 km²)

93 mi² (242 km²)

1,405 mi² (3,640 km²)

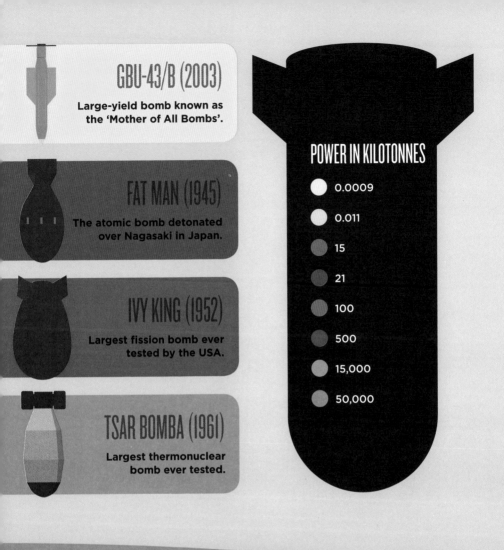

GBU-43/B (2003)

Large-yield bomb known as the 'Mother of All Bombs'.

FAT MAN (1945)

The atomic bomb detonated over Nagasaki in Japan.

IVY KING (1952)

Largest fission bomb ever tested by the USA.

TSAR BOMBA (1961)

Largest thermonuclear bomb ever tested.

POWER IN KILOTONNES

- 0.0009
- 0.011
- 15
- 21
- 100
- 500
- 15,000
- 50,000

0.01 mi² (0.03 km²)

5.9 mi² (15.4 km²)

98 mi² (254 km²)

4,363 mi² (11,300 km²)

The Second World War had a huge and irreversible impact on science. With the disc[overy] of nuclear fission and the development of the concept of nuclear chain reactions in [the] 930s, the creation of an atomic bomb during the war was only a matter of time. At [the same time, Germany was producing rocket equipment that would later form the core technology for the development of space science in the USA and USSR.

The word 'nuclear' often has negative connotations, due to its immense destructive p[ower] [b]ut the development of nuclear fission has also had significant benefits for human[ity].

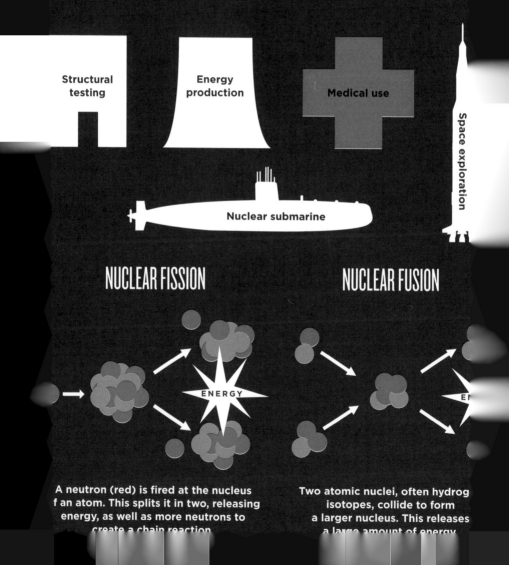

Structural testing

Energy production

Medical use

Space exploration

Nuclear submarine

NUCLEAR FISSION

NUCLEAR FUSION

ENERGY

A neutron (red) is fired at the nucleus [o]f an atom. This splits it in two, releasing energy, as well as more neutrons to create a chain reaction.

Two atomic nuclei, often hydrog[en] isotopes, collide to form a larger nucleus. This releases a large amount of energy.

TIMELINE OF THE ATOMIC BOMB

London, UK
Hungarian physicist Leo Szilard comes up with the concept of a nuclear chain reaction.

Berlin, Germany
German chemists Otto Hahn and Fritz Strassmann publish a report on successful nuclear fission.

Stockholm, Sweden
Austrian physicists Lise Meitner and Otto Frisch publish a theory of nuclear fission including the potential for nuclear weapons.

Washington, D.C., USA
President Franklin Roosevelt receives a letter from Einstein and Szilard pointing out the risk of German nuclear weapons and the need for the USA to develop them.

Berlin, Germany
The German nuclear power project is split into three areas: uranium and heavy water production, uranium isotope separation and the Uranmaschine (uranium machine).

Washington, D.C., USA
President Franklin Roosevelt approves an atomic programme.

Manhattan, USA
Liaison office for the Army side of the US project established and given the name 'Manhattan Project'.

Berlin, Germany
The German nuclear weapon programme begins to wind down in favour of more pressing war-related projects. Germany refocuses the use of nuclear power for energy.

Peenemünde, Germany
The first V-2 ballistic missile is launched on London – this would form the starting point for the US and USSR space race.

Alamogordo, USA
The first successful atomic bomb is detonated in Trinity test.

Hiroshima, Japan
The uranium-based Little Boy bomb is dropped.

Nagasaki, Japan
The plutonium-based Fat Man bomb is dropped.

| 1930 |
| 1931 |
| 1932 |
| 1933 |
| 1934 |
| 1935 |
| 1936 |
| 1937 |
| 1938 |
| 1939 |
| 1940 |
| 1941 |
| 1942 |
| 1943 |
| 1944 |
| 1945 |
| 1946 |
| 1947 |
| 1948 |
| 1949 |
| 1950 |

SCIENTIFIC EXODUS

In the 1920s, the German state had a mixed attitude to Einstein. On the one hand, he was the great German scientist who was fêted around the world for his general theory of relativity. On the other hand, he was Jewish and clearly unpatriotic, as he had renounced his German citizenship. Nothing better illustrates this dual attitude than when the city of Berlin celebrated Einstein's 50th birthday by giving him a house near the river Havel, while at the same time the German authorities were criticizing his 'Jewish physics'. Before he moved to the USA, Einstein would put considerable effort into visiting other countries to encourage the authorities to take in refugee scientists (not all Jews) and their families.

Physicists who moved countries in the 1930s due to Hitler's rise to power:

ALBERT EINSTEIN
Born in Germany, Einstein visited the UK to encourage the government to extract Jewish scientists from Germany. He travelled to the USA in 1933, and gained citizenship in 1940.

MAX BORN
Born left his country of birth, Germany, in 1933 and travelled to the UK with a brief stay in India. He was given British citizenship in 1939.

ERWIN SCHRÖDINGER
Schrödinger was born in Austria and taught in Germany. Like Einstein he headed for the UK, but moved to Ireland where he became a citizen in 1948.

NIELS BOHR
With Denmark occupied by the Nazis, he left his homeland for the UK, via Sweden, in 1943. In the same year, he visited Einstein and Wolfgang Pauli in the USA before returning to Denmark in 1945.

EINSTEIN

50

ENRICO FERMI

Fermi was born in Italy and travelled to Sweden to collect his Nobel Prize. He did not return home and instead took up a position at Columbia University in the USA. He was made a US citizen in 1944.

LISE MEITNER

Born in Austria-Hungary, Meitner was the first female professor in physics at the University of Berlin. She fled Germany for the Netherlands in 1938. In the same year, she moved to Sweden and was made a citizen in 1949.

OTTO FRISCH

Frisch moved regularly. He was born in Austria-Hungary and educated in Germany. He left the country as Hitler was appointed Chancellor. In 1943, he received British citizenship.

WOLFGANG PAULI

Austrian-born Pauli taught in Switzerland, but with the outbreak of war he was forced to move to the USA. He became a naturalized citizen of the USA, but returned to Switzerland in 1946.

HANS BETHE

Bethe left Germany in 1933 after Jewish scientists were banned from academic positions. He taught in the UK and in the USA. He was given US citizenship in 1941.

EDWARD TELLER

With Hitler's rise to power, Austria-Hungarian-born Teller fled Germany for the UK in 1933. He emigrated to the USA in 1935 and was made a citizen in 1941.

5 THINGS YOU DIDN'T KNOW ABOUT ALBERT EINSTEIN

1 When Einstein's sister was born, his mother had promised him "something new to play with". He was disappointed to see a baby and asked, "Where are the wheels?"

2 Einstein never wore socks, his reason being: "When I was young, I found out that the big toe always ends up making a hole in a sock. So I stopped wearing socks.'

3 After moving to the US, Einstein owned a 15-foot dinghy called *Tinef*, Yiddish for 'worthless'. He was not a very accomplished sailor and he never learnt to swim, resulting in him being rescued on numerous occasions.

4 Einstein spent several weeks in the UK in 1933, meeting Winston Churchill and encouraging support for Jewish scientists in Germany. He later organized a rally at the Royal Albert Hall in London where he raised $500,000 for The Academic Assistance Council, which assisted in the retrieval of scholars from Germany.

5 In his old age, Einstein once forgot his address and rang up his office to check what it was. But they had instructions not to give the address out, to prevent Einstein from being bothered, so they initially refused to tell him.

ALBERT EINSTEIN

03
WORK

"THE WHOLE DEVELOPMENT OF THE THEORY [OF RELATIVITY] TURNS ON THE QUESTION OF WHETHER THERE ARE PHYSICALLY PREFERRED STATES OF MOTION IN NATURE."

—Albert Einstein, lecture delivered to the Nordic Assembly of Naturalists, Gothenburg, 1923

CURRICULUM VITAE

WORK EXPERIENCE:

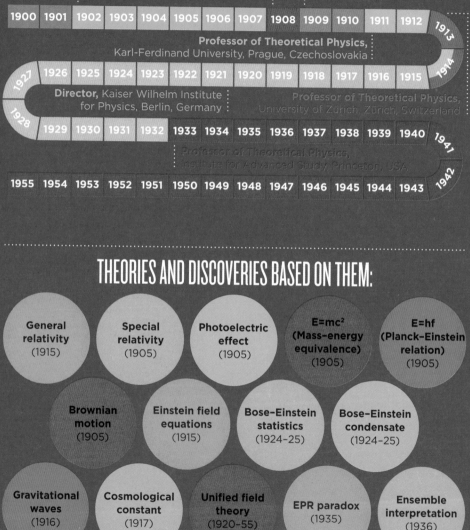

Associate Professor, University of Bern, Bern, Switzerland

Assistant Examiner, Federal Office for Intellectual Property, Bern, Switzerland

Associate Professor of Theoretical Physics, University of Zürich, Zürich, Switzerland

| 1900 | 1901 | 1902 | 1903 | 1904 | 1905 | 1906 | 1907 | 1908 | 1909 | 1910 | 1911 | 1912 | 1913 |

Professor of Theoretical Physics, Karl-Ferdinand University, Prague, Czechoslovakia

| 1927 | 1926 | 1925 | 1924 | 1923 | 1922 | 1921 | 1920 | 1919 | 1918 | 1917 | 1916 | 1915 | 1914 |

Director, Kaiser Wilhelm Institute for Physics, Berlin, Germany

Professor of Theoretical Physics, University of Zürich, Zürich, Switzerland

| 1928 | 1929 | 1930 | 1931 | 1932 | 1933 | 1934 | 1935 | 1936 | 1937 | 1938 | 1939 | 1940 | 1941 |

Professor of Theoretical Physics, Institute for Advanced Study, Princeton, USA

| 1955 | 1954 | 1953 | 1952 | 1951 | 1950 | 1949 | 1948 | 1947 | 1946 | 1945 | 1944 | 1943 | 1942 |

THEORIES AND DISCOVERIES BASED ON THEM:

General relativity (1915)

Special relativity (1905)

Photoelectric effect (1905)

$E=mc^2$ (Mass-energy equivalence) (1905)

$E=hf$ (Planck–Einstein relation) (1905)

Brownian motion (1905)

Einstein field equations (1915)

Bose-Einstein statistics (1924–25)

Bose-Einstein condensate (1924–25)

Gravitational waves (1916)

Cosmological constant (1917)

Unified field theory (1920–55)

EPR paradox (1935)

Ensemble interpretation (1936)

PUBLISHED PAPERS: 300+

KEY YEAR: 1905

Most mathematicians and scientists reach a peak when they are young. Einstein certainly had a remarkable year in 1905, when he was 26, but had a longer span of creative activity than most in his field.

CITIZENSHIPS GAINED:

1901 Swiss

1914 German (renounced in 1933)

1940 US

KEY PAPERS:

- *On a Heuristic Point of View Concerning the Production and Transformation of Light,* **March 1905**
  Nobel Prize winning theory

- *A New Determination of Molecular Dimensions*, **April 1905**
  PhD thesis

- *Zur Elektrodynamik bewegter Körper* (*On the Electrodynamics of Moving Bodies*), **June 1905**
  The special theory of relativity

- *Ist die Trägheit eines Körpers von seinem Energieinhalt abhängig? (Does the Inertia of a Body Depend on its Energy Content?*), **September 1905**
  A short paper based on special relativity showing that $E=mc^2$

LANGUAGES SPOKEN:

German

English

REFERENCES:

Alfred Kleiner

Heinrich Friedrich Weber

WORK

57

CITATION NOT NEEDED

NUMBER OF CITATIONS OF EINSTEIN'S PAPERS:

NOBEL PRIZE

DOCTORAL DISSERTATION (1905) — 3,440

BROWNIAN MOTION/EXISTENCE OF ATOMS (1905) — 8,577

PHOTOELECTRIC EFFECT/QUANTUM PHYSICS (1905) — 10,026

SPECIAL THEORY OF RELATIVITY (1905) — 1,025

$E=mc^2$ (1905) — 304

There is not another scientist in history who achieved so much in a single year as Einstein did in 1905. At the time, he was working in the Swiss patent office in Bern and had no academic status. And yet, as well as completing his doctorate, he managed to publish four papers that between them would represent more than a lifetime's work for many scientists. The papers confirmed the existence of atoms, explained the photoelectric effect using quantum theory (the paper that won him the Nobel Prize), established the special theory of relativity and pointed out that $E=mc^2$. Einstein's papers were relatively infrequently referred to by others. Frequently cited papers tend to have practical methods in them; Einstein's theories were so fundamental they are rarely considered in need of a citation.

MOST CITATIONS OF OTHERS, AS LISTED BY *NATURE* IN 2014:

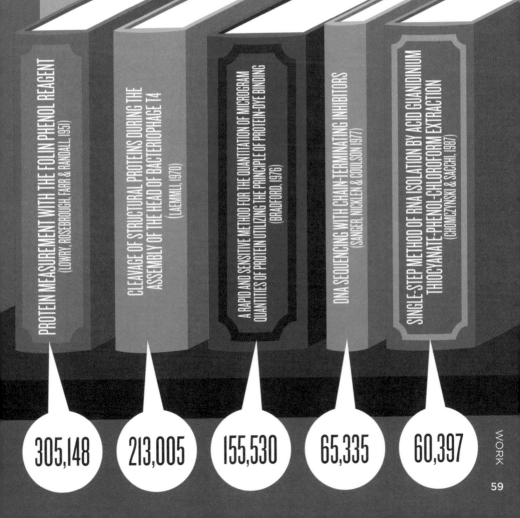

PROTEIN MEASUREMENT WITH THE FOLIN PHENOL REAGENT
(LOWRY, ROSEBROUGH, FARR & RANDALL, 1951)

305,148

CLEAVAGE OF STRUCTURAL PROTEINS DURING THE ASSEMBLY OF THE HEAD OF BACTERIOPHAGE T4
(LAEMMLI, 1970)

213,005

A RAPID AND SENSITIVE METHOD FOR THE QUANTITATION OF MICROGRAM QUANTITIES OF PROTEIN UTILIZING THE PRINCIPLE OF PROTEIN-DYE BINDING
(BRADFORD, 1976)

155,530

DNA SEQUENCING WITH CHAIN-TERMINATING INHIBITORS
(SANGER, NICKLEN & COULSON 1977)

65,335

SINGLE-STEP METHOD OF RNA ISOLATION BY ACID GUANIDINIUM THIOCYANATE-PHENOL-CHLOROFORM EXTRACTION
(CHOMCZYNSKI & SACCHI, 1987)

60,397

Danish physicist Niels Bohr was a long-time friend of Einstein's – but the pair had a radically dissimilar approach to their work. The differences between them particularly came out when they met at a number of conferences in the 1920s and 1930s when Einstein would delight in finding thought experiments to challenge Bohr's support for quantum physics. In a typical encounter, Einstein would set Bohr a challenge over breakfast, which would leave Bohr struggling to come up with an answer through the day, only to come back at teatime with a grin to show the mistake that Einstein had made.

EINSTEIN

NAMED AFTER EINSTEIN

- **Asteroid: 2001 Einstein**
- **Einstein lunar crater**
- **Element: einsteinium**

COUNTRY

Gave up his German citizenship and considered himself, if anything, a citizen of the world.

OUTSIDE SCIENCE

Best known for music, notably the violin.

NOBEL PRIZE
1921

FAMILY

Married to Mileva for 16 years and to Elsa for 17 years. Family always came second. He had three children: one girl and two boys.

PASSING ON THE SCIENCE

His son Hans Albert became a professor of hydraulic engineering.

ALBERT EINSTEIN (1879 – 1955)

BOHR

The account of their disputes was written up in 1949 by Bohr in an article entitled *Discussions with Einstein on Epistemological Problems in Atomic Physics*. Despite their differing opinions, they each held the other in high regard.

NIELS BOHR (1885 – 1962)

COUNTRY

A proud Dane, who made Copenhagen a centre for quantum physics research.

NAMED AFTER BOHR

- Asteroid: 3948 Bohr
- Bohr lunar crater
- Element: bohrium

OUTSIDE SCIENCE

Best known for sport, notably football.

FAMILY

A family man, Bohr was married for 50 years to Margrethe and had six children, all boys.

NOBEL PRIZE
1922

PASSING ON THE SCIENCE

His son Aage won the Nobel Prize in Physics for work on atomic nuclei.

MOLECULES EXIST

In 1827, Scottish botanist Robert Brown noticed that tiny particles from pollen grains would dance around in water as if they were alive, but he didn't know why. Nearly 80 years later, in the first of his great papers of 1905, Einstein not only explained this as the result of constant collision from water molecules but also used data to produce a mathematical model of the process that gave an idea of the relative scale of water molecules. This was very significant as it was one of the first clear pieces of evidence that atoms and molecules existed.

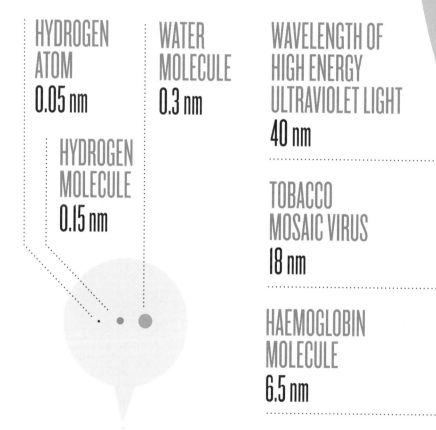

HYDROGEN ATOM
0.05 nm

WATER MOLECULE
0.3 nm

WAVELENGTH OF HIGH ENERGY ULTRAVIOLET LIGHT
40 nm

HYDROGEN MOLECULE
0.15 nm

TOBACCO MOSAIC VIRUS
18 nm

HAEMOGLOBIN MOLECULE
6.5 nm

1 nanometre = one billionth of a metre (0.000000001 m)

SIZE COMPARISONS IN NANOMETRES (nm)

WAVELENGTH OF GREEN LIGHT
540 nm

TOBACCO SMOKE PARTICLE
200 nm

TYPICAL VIRUS
100 nm

Most molecules are far too small to be seen by the naked eye. But under a microscope their difference in size can be measured.

QUANTUM FOUNDATIONS

THE ELECTROMAGNETIC SPECTRUM

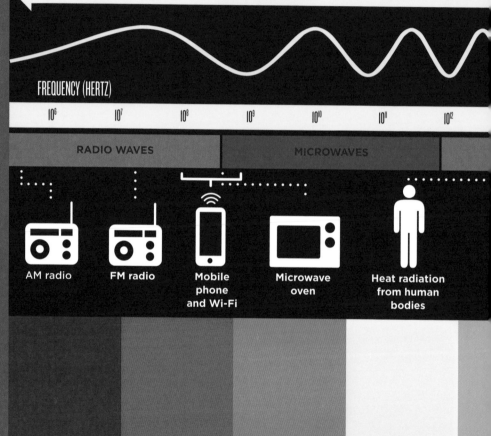

⟵ INCREASING WAVELENGTH

FREQUENCY (HERTZ)

| 10^6 | 10^7 | 10^8 | 10^9 | 10^{10} | 10^{11} | 10^{12} |

RADIO WAVES | **MICROWAVES**

AM radio

FM radio

Mobile phone and Wi-Fi

Microwave oven

Heat radiation from human bodies

The graphic shows the energies of photons in the electromagnetic spectrum, with the equivalent scale of waves. The amount of energy is directly proportional to the photon's frequency and inversely proportional to the wavelength. The higher the frequency, the higher its energy. Consequently, the longer the wavelength,

The paper that won Einstein the Nobel Prize would ironically help to found quantum physics, the science he came to distrust. It was known that shining a light on some metals produced an electric current – the photoelectric effect..If light were a wave, you would expect that the bigger the wave, the bigger the current. But some colours of light produced no electricity, no matter how intense the light. Einstein realized this would be the case if light were made of quantum particles – photons – whose energy determined the colour of the light. Only if a photon had enough energy could it knock out an electron to start an electric current.

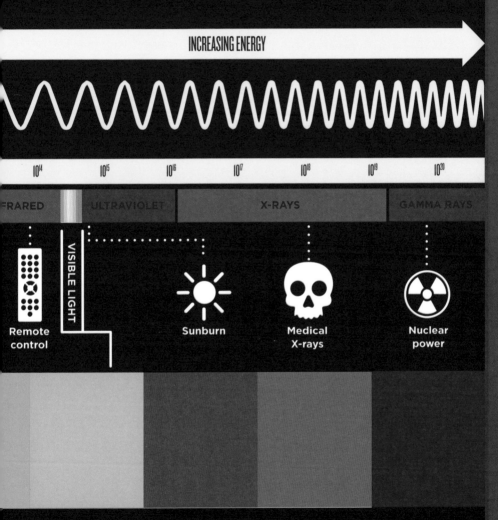

INCREASING ENERGY

10^{14} 10^{15} 10^{16} 10^{17} 10^{18} 10^{19} 10^{20}

FRARED   ULTRAVIOLET   X-RAYS   GAMMA RAYS

VISIBLE LIGHT

Remote
control

Sunburn

Medical
X-rays

Nuclear
power

the lower its energy. Red light is produced by photons with low energy, long wavelengths and low frequency, whereas violet light is produced by photons with high energy, short wavelengeths and high frequency.

SPECIAL RELATIVITY

The work that would always be most identified with Einstein was part of his remarkable 1905 output. His special theory of relativity combined Newton's laws of motion with the discovery that light could only exist if it travelled at a specific speed. The requirement that light moved at the same speed however you moved with respect to it inextricably linked time and space. This means that a moving body would shrink in the direction of movement, increase in mass and have its time slow down. In the last of four papers published in 1905, Einstein introduced $m=E/c^2$ (where m=mass, E=energy and c^2=speed of light squared) but added that mass and energy were interchangeable, leading to $E=mc^2$, the world's most famous equation. While it's hard to grasp the importance of just the equation, Einstein connected two seemingly unrelated components, mass and energy. This is now used to explain everything from the Big Bang to the atomic bomb.

SPECIAL RELATIVITY IN EFFECT

Time slows down or speeds up depending on how fast you move relative to something else. The closer your speed gets to the speed of light, the slower time goes, though you wouldn't notice its effect until you returned back to the original stationary position. Approaching the speed of light, a person inside a spaceship would age much slower than those left at home. The graphic show the time difference for some real and hypothetical travellers moving at differing speeds, compared to someone stationary on Earth.

$$E = mc^2$$

energy   mass   speed of light squared

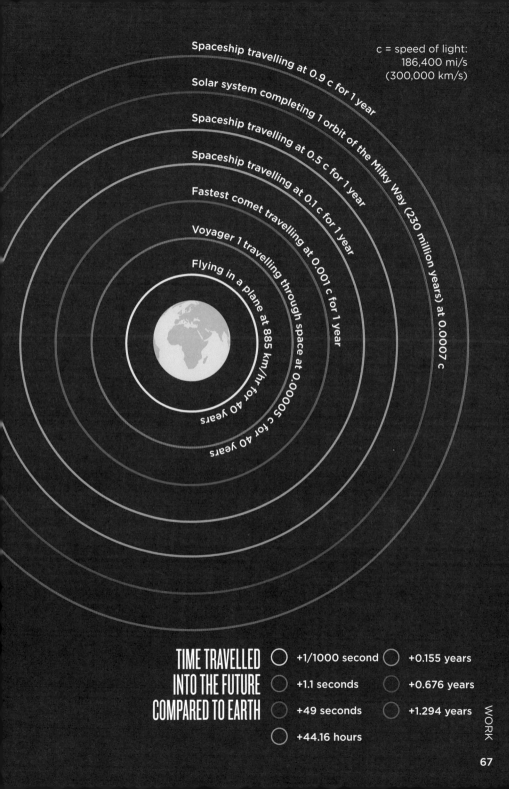

Spaceship travelling at 0.9 c for 1 year

c = speed of light:
186,400 mi/s
(300,000 km/s)

Solar system completing 1 orbit of the Milky Way (230 million years) at 0.0007 c

Spaceship travelling at 0.5 c for 1 year

Spaceship travelling at 0.1 c for 1 year

Fastest comet travelling at 0.001 c for 1 year

Voyager 1 travelling through space at 0.00005 c for 40 years

Flying in a plane at 885 km/hr for 40 years

**TIME TRAVELLED
INTO THE FUTURE
COMPARED TO EARTH**

⭕ +1/1000 second ⭕ +0.155 years

⭕ +1.1 seconds ⭕ +0.676 years

⭕ +49 seconds ⭕ +1.294 years

⭕ +44.16 hours

THE GENERAL THEORY OF RELATIVITY

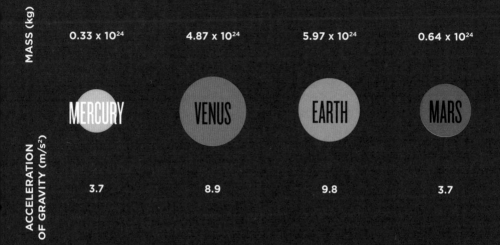

MASS (kg)

| 0.33 x 10^{24} | 4.87 x 10^{24} | 5.97 x 10^{24} | 0.64 x 10^{24} |

MERCURY   VENUS   EARTH   MARS

ACCELERATION
OF GRAVITY (m/s^2)

| 3.7 | 8.9 | 9.8 | 3.7 |

The special theory of relativity was given the term special, not because it was remarkable (though it was) but because it was limited to special cases. While still working at the patent office, Einstein realized that if he fully brought acceleration into the picture, it would enable the theory to do far more. This was because acceleration and gravity were indistinguishable. By generalizing his theory, he could provide an explanation for why matter caused gravitation – because it warped space and time – and how warped space and time changed the way matter moved. The general theory proved mathematically highly challenging, but Einstein persevered and published a groundbreaking theory.

Matter warps space and time. The greater the mass, the more this warping occurs (in the extreme, a black hole warps spacetime so much that even light cannot escape). A massive body, such as a planet, warps the spacetime around it and influences other objects. A free-falling object on Earth has an acceleration of 9.8 m/s², whereas on other planets their differing masses result in differences in acceleration.

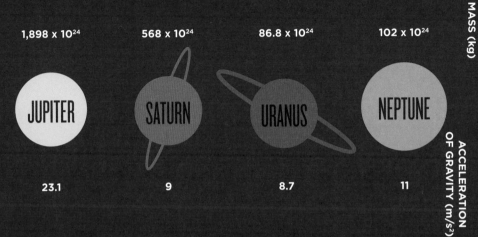

MASS (kg)

$1,898 \times 10^{24}$ 568×10^{24} 86.8×10^{24} 102×10^{24}

JUPITER   SATURN   URANUS   NEPTUNE

ACCELERATION OF GRAVITY (m/s²)

23.1   9   8.7   11

MODELLING THE UNIVERSE

The general theory of relativity was a triumph, providing a more accurate description of gravity than Newton's, but it soon proved capable of far more. Just a few weeks after its publication, German physicist Karl Schwarzschild solved Einstein's equations for a spherical body, making the first prediction of what would become known as a black hole. The following year, Dutch physicist Willem de Sitter applied the theory to the universe as a whole. Though his was a simplistic, empty universe, it was the first of many attempts to use general relativity to describe the behaviour of the universe, leading to the current "big bang" theory.

OVER THE YEARS, AS WE HAVE FOUND OUT MORE ABOUT IT, OUR UNDERSTANDING OF THE SIZE OF THE UNIVERSE HAS SHIFTED MANY TIMES:

- 0.0002 light years – Archimedes (3rd century BC) – Earth-centred universe

- 0.00003 light years – Ptolemy (2nd century AD) – Earth-centred universe

- 0.2 light years – Tycho Brahe (16th century AD) – Copernican universe

- 2 light years – Aristarchus, via Archimedes (3rd century BC) – Sun-centred universe

- 8,000 light years – William Herschel (18th/19th century)

- 100,000 light years – Harlow Shapley (20th century)

- 6 billion light years – Edwin Hubble (20th century)

- 90 billion light years – Current observable universe (21st century)

- infinite – Isaac Newton (17th/18th century)

Due to the vastness of space, it is not practical to measure distances in small units such as miles and kilometres. A light year is the distance that light can travel in a year. To convert this to miles, you take the speed of light (186,000 miles per second) multiplied by the number of seconds in an hour (3,600) multiplied by the number of hours in a day (24) multiplied by the number days in a year (365).

186,000 x 3,600 x 24 x 365 = 5,878,625,373,184 miles

1
light
year

=

6
trillion miles
(10 trillion
km)

GRAVITATIONAL WAVES

In 1916, his mind full of the implications of the general theory of relativity, Einstein proposed that moving bodies would generate gravitational waves – compression and stretching of spacetime itself. By 1936, though, working with Nathan Rosen at Princeton, he became convinced they didn't exist at all … only to correct his paper one year later, bringing them back. Even then, he believed that gravitational waves were so faint they would never be detected. However, in September 2015, 100 years after the general theory was published, gravitational waves were detected by the US-based Laser Interferometer Gravitational-Wave Observatory (LIGO), ushering in a new era of astronomy.

WHAT HAPPENS WHEN TWO BLACK HOLES COLLIDE?

When two black holes are in close proximity, it becomes impossible for them to avoid each other's gravity. The result is that they spiral towards each other and eventually collide, forming one even larger black hole. Such an event is extremely violent and produces a large amount of energy in the form of gravitational waves, which affect the curvature of spacetime.

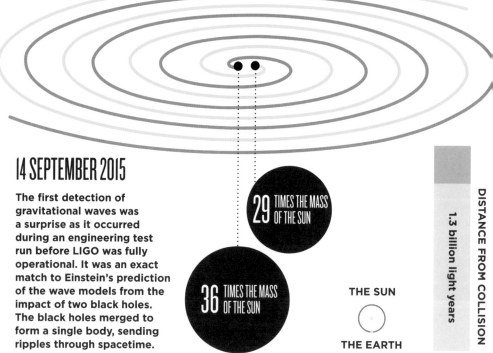

14 SEPTEMBER 2015

The first detection of gravitational waves was a surprise as it occurred during an engineering test run before LIGO was fully operational. It was an exact match to Einstein's prediction of the wave models from the impact of two black holes. The black holes merged to form a single body, sending ripples through spacetime.

29 TIMES THE MASS OF THE SUN

36 TIMES THE MASS OF THE SUN

THE SUN

THE EARTH

1.3 billion light years

DISTANCE FROM COLLISION

EINSTEIN

72

WHEN THE TWO BLACK HOLES COLLIDED PEAK POWER WAS MEASURED AT 200 SOLAR MASSES PER SECOND, WHICH IS 50 TIMES THE TOTAL OUTPUT POWER OF ALL THE STARS IN THE OBSERVABLE UNIVERSE

= one solar mass

QUANTUM ENTANGLEMENT

Attempting to discredit quantum theory, Einstein produced his last major contribution to physics in 1935. In a paper written with Boris Podolsky and Nathan Rosen, Einstein showed that quantum theory made it possible for two particles, in a state called entanglement, to influence each other instantly, even if they are separated at any distance. This apparently contradicted the light speed limit of relativity. The paper concluded that either quantum physics was wrong or it was necessary to throw away the concept of 'local reality', whereby an object is only directly influenced by its immediate surroundings. This became known as the Einstein-Podolsky-Rosen (EPR) paradox. This was intended to be a death blow for quantum physics, but in practice, entanglement has been shown to work and Einstein was proved wrong.

*graphic not to scale

THE INCREASING DISTANCE ENTANGLEMENT HAS BEEN DEMONSTRATED OVER

Quantum entanglement occurs when two particles become linked as if they were two parts of the same object and remain connected over a distance so that any action performed on one particle also has an effect on the other. The first proven instance of entanglement occurred in 1972, and since then scientists have experimented at ever increasing distances. The importance of this testing is that entanglement makes it possible to generate unbreakable ciphers and is essential in making quantum computers work.

3.2 feet (1 m) Stuart Freedman and John Clauser, Berkeley, California (1972)

1,968 feet (600 m) Anton Zeilinger, Vienna, Austria (2003)

8 miles (13 km) Pan Jian-Wei, Heifei, China (2004)

9.4 miles (15.2 km) Anton Zeilinger, Vienna, Austria (2004)

9.9 miles (16 km) Pan Jian-Wei, Great Wall of China (2009)

89 miles (143 km) Anton Zeilinger, Canary islands: La Palma to Tenerife (2012)

870 miles (1,400 km) Pan Jian-Wei, Earth to satellite to Earth (2017)

5 THINGS YOU DIDN'T KNOW ABOUT EINSTEIN'S WORK

1 Although Einstein's name will always be linked to relativity, it was Galileo who first developed the basics of relativity. Einstein's special and general theories built on this to add in the relationship of time and space (special theory), and the relationship between matter and spacetime (general theory).

2 In 1921, the Nobel Committee for Physics decided that none of the nominations had met the standard for the award. In such circumstances, the presentation of the prize can be delayed by a year. So Einstein actually won the 1921 award in 1922.

3 When Einstein submitted his thesis on the size of molecules, he was told it was too short. He added one sentence before resubmitting, when it was promptly accepted.

4 In 1926, Einstein and fellow physicist Leo Szilard patented a new kind of refrigerator that wouldn't leak toxic coolants, which was a risk with early fridges.

5 When gravitational waves were discovered in 2015, headlines proclaimed "Einstein proved right" – but it was actually "Einstein proved wrong". Although he first predicted gravitational waves in 1916, he later said that they would be impossible to ever detect.

EINSTEIN PROVED RIGHT!

ALBERT EINSTEIN

04
LEGACY

"ONE THING I HAVE LEARNED IN A LONG LIFE: THAT ALL OUR SCIENCE, MEASURED AGAINST REALITY, IS PRIMITIVE AND CHILDLIKE — AND YET IT IS THE MOST PRECIOUS THING WE HAVE."

—Albert Einstein, *Albert Einstein: Creator and Rebel*, 1972

THE TROPHY CABINET

Although other prizes tend to be overshadowed by the Nobel, Einstein was showered with accolades once he became famous after the publication of his general theory of relativity. As well as the medals and trophies, Einstein received a house near the river Havel from the city of Berlin on his 50th birthday and later was offered the position of second president of Israel, which he felt unable to accept.

1913
Member of Prussian Academy of Sciences

1920
Barnard Medal

1923
Admitted to 'Pour le Mérite' (German order for science or art)

1926
Gold Medal of the Royal Astronomical Society, London

1929
Max Planck Medal (German Physical Society)

1931
Prix Jules Janssen (French Astronomical Society)

1925
Copley Medal (Royal Society)

1921

Nobel Prize
in Physics
(awarded
in 1922)

1921

Foreign
Member of
the Royal
Society

1923

Genootschap
Medal (Dutch
Scientific
Society)

1921

Matteucci Medal
(Italian physics
award)

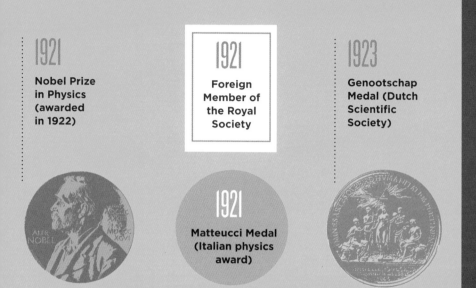

1935

Franklin Medal
(Physics award
from the Franklin
Institute,
Philadelphia)

1955

Element einsteinium
named after him

1999

Time magazine Person
of the Century

99

Es

Einsteinium

TIME

ALBERT
EINSTEIN

FAMILY TREE OF SCIENCE

When faced with a genius like Einstein it can be easy to see him entirely in isolation – yet any scientist, however great, builds on the work of others. Newton famously wrote to philosopher Robert Hooke, "If I have seen further it is by standing on the shoulders of giants" – although there is evidence that he was being sarcastic about Hooke, who was short in height, after the two began to disagree. But the sentiment rings true across the ages. Einstein was not great at crediting others, but there is no doubt of his many influencers – nor of the scientists he would himself influence.

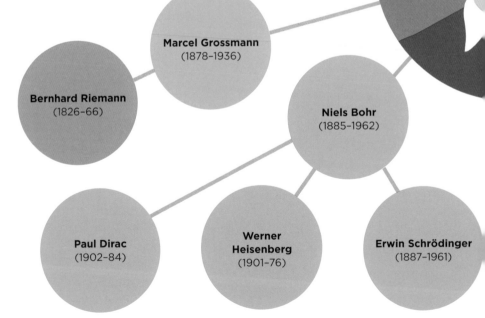

Isaac Newton
(1642–1727)

Michael Faraday
(1791–1867)

Max Planck
(1858–1947)

Marcel Grossmann
(1878–1936)

Bernhard Riemann
(1826–66)

Niels Bohr
(1885–1962)

Paul Dirac
(1902–84)

Werner Heisenberg
(1901–76)

Erwin Schrödinger
(1887–1961)

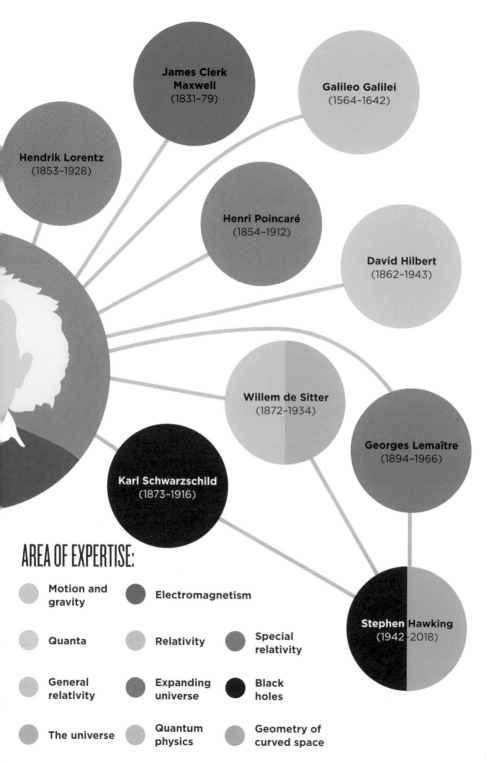

James Clerk Maxwell (1831–79)

Galileo Galilei (1564–1642)

Hendrik Lorentz (1853–1928)

Henri Poincaré (1854–1912)

David Hilbert (1862–1943)

Willem de Sitter (1872–1934)

Georges Lemaître (1894–1966)

Karl Schwarzschild (1873–1916)

AREA OF EXPERTISE:

Motion and gravity

Electromagnetism

Quanta

Relativity

Special relativity

General relativity

Expanding universe

Black holes

The universe

Quantum physics

Geometry of curved space

Stephen Hawking (1942–2018)

GPS & RELATIVITY

It's easy to think of the special and general theories of relativity as being abstract science without practical applications – but there are circumstances where they have to be brought into consideration, and nowhere is this more obvious than in the GPS satellite system used for satellite navigation. Each GPS satellite is effectively an incredibly accurate clock, constantly pumping out the time. But special relativity means that the moving clock time runs slow compared to the Earth's surface, while general relativity shows lower gravity makes them run fast. If the composite correction were not applied, a satnav's apparent position would drift by several miles a day.

+45 MICRO-SECONDS

Effect of general relativity over a 24-hour period on a GPS clock in orbit, compared to one on earth.

-7 MICRO-SECONDS

Effect of special relativity over a 24-hour period on a GPS clock in orbit, compared to one on earth.

5 METRES – LEVEL OF ACCURACY

ALTITUDE
12,550
MILES
(20,000 km)

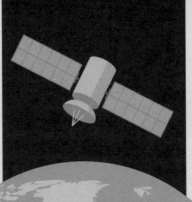

VELOCITY
8,637
MPH
(14,000 km/h)

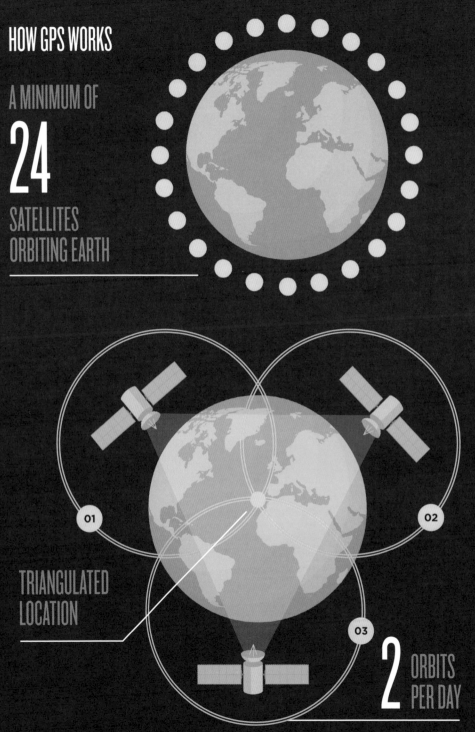

HOW GPS WORKS

A MINIMUM OF
24
SATELLITES
ORBITING EARTH

01

02

03

TRIANGULATED
LOCATION

2 ORBITS
PER DAY

THE RELUCTANT QUANTUM

Quantum theory might seem complicated, but it has many practical applications and it's almost certain there will be technology that required quantum physics in its design within a few feet as you read this. It has been estimated that 35 per cent of GDP in developed countries is due to products and services dependent on quantum physics. Although Einstein spent many years opposing quantum theory because of his dislike of the use of probability, it shouldn't be forgotten that he helped lay the foundations of the field.

ANNUAL INTERNET TRAFFIC:
1.2 THOUSAND BILLION BILLION BYTES

2 BILLION COMPUTERS

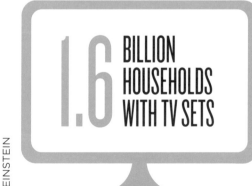
1.6 BILLION HOUSEHOLDS WITH TV SETS

100 BILLION MUSIC STREAMS PER YEAR

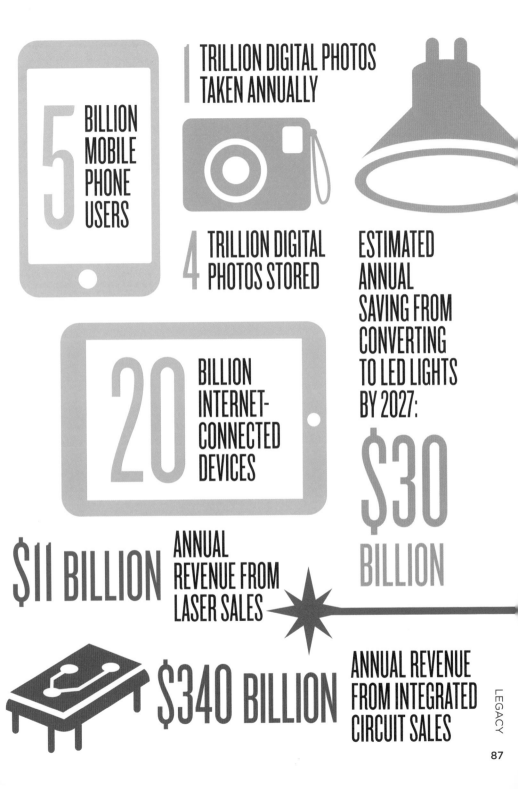

5 BILLION MOBILE PHONE USERS

1 TRILLION DIGITAL PHOTOS TAKEN ANNUALLY

4 TRILLION DIGITAL PHOTOS STORED

20 BILLION INTERNET-CONNECTED DEVICES

ESTIMATED ANNUAL SAVING FROM CONVERTING TO LED LIGHTS BY 2027: **$30 BILLION**

$11 BILLION ANNUAL REVENUE FROM LASER SALES

$340 BILLION ANNUAL REVENUE FROM INTEGRATED CIRCUIT SALES

TYPOGRAPHIC EINSTEIN

It might seem strange that the standout word (other than Einstein's name) in this cloud should be 'light'. However, light was central to the development of the special theory of relativity, to the photoelectric effect that won him the Nobel Prize and is used to detect the warping effect of general relativity. Not surprisingly, 'theory', 'physics', 'relativity', 'gravity' and 'energy' also come through strongly. Another significant appearance, 'time', is influenced by both the special and general theories of relativity.

SMART

ULTRAVIOLET UNIVERSE BRAIN

BLACK HOLE GENIUS

THEORY

MANHATTAN PROJECT

BOSE-EINSTEIN CONDENSATE

PHOTOELECTRIC EFFECT

RELATIVITY

EINS

SUN

NAGASAKI

MOTION

GRAVITATIONAL WAVES

URANIUM

FISSION

TIME

ENERGY

REFRIGERATOR

ULM

IQ

ATOMIC BOMB

VIOLIN

1905

PRINCETON

ELECTROMAGNETISM

UNIFIED FIELD THEORY

QUANTUM

EINSTEIN

SPECIAL RELATIVITY

NOBEL PRIZE INNOVATIVE

RELIGION ISRAEL PACIFIST NEUTRON

GRAVITY GENERAL RELATIVITY COSMOLOGY

LIGHT

TEIN

SOLAR ECLIPSE EQUATION

GALILEO EPR PARADOX

MATHEMATICIAN NUCLEAR $E=mc^2$ ELECTRICITY

PHYSICS

RADIO WAVES UNIVERSE HIROSHIMA SECOND WORLD WAR PATENT OFFICE

AGNOSTIC BORN LETTERS

THEORETICAL PHYSICS BIGGEST MISTAKE

BROWNIAN MOTION

US CITIZENSHIP

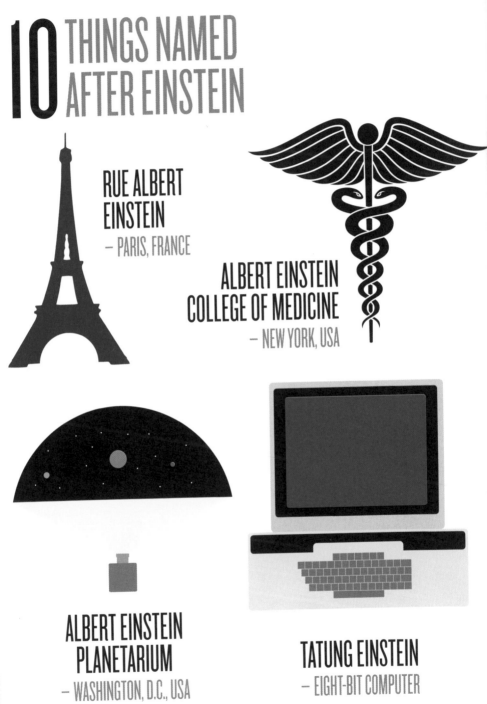

10 THINGS NAMED AFTER EINSTEIN

RUE ALBERT EINSTEIN
– PARIS, FRANCE

ALBERT EINSTEIN COLLEGE OF MEDICINE
– NEW YORK, USA

ALBERT EINSTEIN PLANETARIUM
– WASHINGTON, D.C., USA

TATUNG EINSTEIN
– EIGHT-BIT COMPUTER

EINSTEIN OBSERVATORY
– X-RAY TELESCOPE

ALBERT EINSTEIN ATV
– SUPPLY SPACECRAFT

EINSTEIN CROSS
– QUASAR, DUPLICATED IN THE SKY DUE TO GRAVITATIONAL LENSING

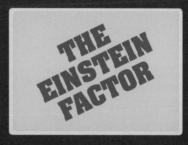

THE EINSTEIN FACTOR
– AUSTRALIAN TELEVISION QUIZ SHOW

EINSTEIN ON THE BEACH
– OPERA BY PHILIP GLASS

EINSTEIN GARGOYLE
– UNIVERSITY OF OREGON, USA

BIOGRAPHIES

Nathan Rosen (1909–95)
Einstein's assistant at the Institute for Advanced Studies, Rosen contributed to much of Einstein's late work, including the EPR paper and the concept of wormholes.

Marcel Grossmann (1878–1936)
A lifetime friend from university days, Grossmann provided Einstein with essential help when it came to the complex mathematics required for general relativity.

Mileva Marić (1875–1948)
In Albert's early years, Mileva, who also studied physics, was a sounding board for his ideas, but as he travelled more, their relationship deteriorated, leading to divorce.

Helen Dukas (1896–1982)
Born in Germany, Dukas became Einstein's secretary in 1928 and accompanied him to Princeton, adding housekeeper to her duties after Elsa's death.

Hermann Einstein (1847–1902)
Albert's father enjoyed mathematics at school, but his business ventures were rarely great successes. However, with wife Pauline, he provided Albert with a stable upbringing.

Max Born (1882–1970)
German physicist and a good friend of the Einstein family, Born developed the probabilistic aspect of quantum physics that Einstein so disliked.

Hans Albert Einstein (1904–73)
Like his parents, Hans Albert studied at the ETH, though he then worked as an engineer. He moved in 1938 to the USA, where he would become a professor.

Elsa Einstein (1876–1936)
A totally different character to Mileva, Elsa was content to play the caring wife. She was both first and second cousin to Albert (her maiden name was Einstein).

Max Planck (1858–1947)
A leading German physicist, Planck took the first steps in the quantum revolution Albert would help to start. Planck supported Albert's move into German academic circles.

Max Talmud (1869–1941)
Also known as Talmey, Talmud was a Polish medical student whom the Einsteins befriended when Albert was 10. His stories of science helped inspire Albert.

Niels Bohr (1885–1962)
The Danish leader of quantum physics. A total contrast of personality with Albert, Bohr was both a friend and a constant target for Albert's assault on quantum theory.

Maja Einstein (1881–1951)
Albert's only sibling, Maria (always known as Maja) was a close friend for her growing brother. She moved to Princeton, following Albert, in 1939.

friend   colleague

wife   family

INDEX

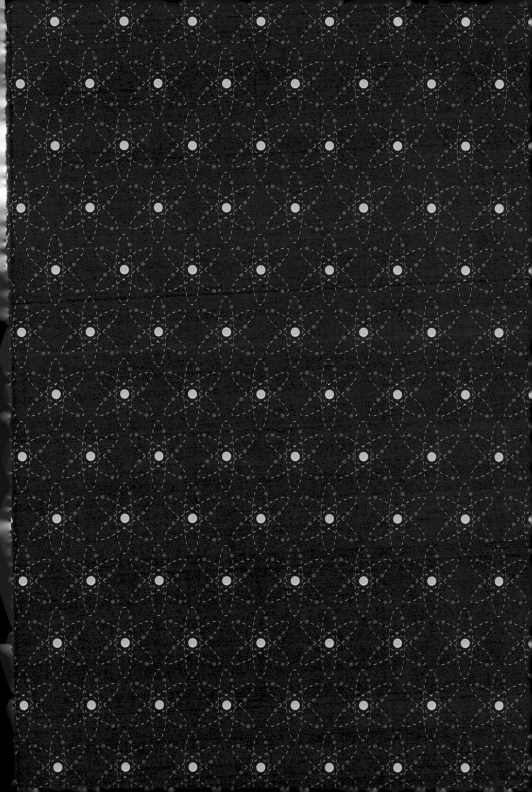